Copyright © 2020 Phoebe Young

All rights reserved.

ISBN: 9798561270727

To my Dad,

The gift of the story you never got to write.

I love you endlessly.

A Journey

THE

GIFT

Guided by Simon Gale

Written by Phoebe Young

CONTENTS

The Beginning – The White Sands of Earth   1

Chapter One   5

Chapter Two   13

Chapter Three   19

Chapter Four   25

Chapter Five   31

Chapter Six   39

Chapter Seven   45

Chapter Eight   53

Chapter Nine   59

Chapter Ten   65

Chapter Eleven   71

Chapter Twelve   77

The End – The White Sands of Heaven   85

My Final Word   89

I Am Free - Poem   91

Prayer of St Francis   93

A Day in Heart Kitchen - Simon's Recipe   95

INTRODUCTION

I want to start by saying thank you for picking up this book today. I can't tell you how much it means to me to be able to share this story with you all.

The story of how I came to write this book began after my dad passed away in 2019. My dad, as so many of our dads, was an incredible man. He was my hero. He had a huge passion for life, a zest and thirst to embrace every opportunity. He was crazy about food and the art of cooking from the heart and inspired many others to do the same. Although he was very unwell for 3 years, he still found the gift in each and every moment, even up until his last day. I have the most precious memories of him, ones that we made together over the last 30 years and those memories are now what keeps him with me, alive in my heart, still surrounded by so much love.

I sat one day by my laptop, overwhelmed by my grief, by the deep ache I am now left with, in the absence of my dad. They say a part of you dies, when the ones you love most depart this world and for me a part really did. I sat thinking and I spoke "How can I share all you taught me, how can I spread your message with others." A message to me that felt so important, a wisdom shared about embracing life as it is and immersing yourself fully into the moment…..when I heard him. It was clear, I could hear his words, I could feel his wisdom and I began to write.

You'll see from the front cover, it's written 'Guided by Simon Gale' and that to me, is how this book came to be. Working with my dad, from another place, a new place, but still so clear with his message.

Life is full of gifts, if we take the time to notice.

Thank you again for reading this book, spread his message far and wide, use it as your own gift. After all, to live a life full of gratitude and love is a life well lived.

EACH DAY WE ARE BORN AGAIN. WHAT WE DO TODAY MATTERS MOST

BUDDHA

THE BEGINNING - THE WHITE SANDS OF EARTH

As I stand on the pure white sandy beach, feeling the ground beneath me, I feel my feet and toes covered by the grit of the sand. I hear the soft sound of the pure blue ocean. The sea hums a gentle song to me, a song that gives me comfort. I feel at home with it. I look to my side. I see my wife and grown children swimming in the crystal-clear water. The laughter, the love they share fills every space in my heart with utter joy. I look down to my feet and I see my grandson, Leo, building his creation in the sand. He has a fire, a determination; anything is possible for Leo and in his presence, anything is possible for me too. I feel the salty sea water around my ankles and the warmth of the sun on my skin.

I look down at my body, a body I hardly recognise as my own anymore. I feel my scars; evidence of the journey my body has been on for the last three years. I feel my bones grasping onto any fat they can to nourish my body. I feel the weakness. It's something I would always ignore, something I didn't want to feel. I would tell myself "I am strong", but right now, I don't feel strong. I stand and breathe. I think to myself "It's OK to feel weak, Simon", I know that right now in this moment, standing in the ocean with my family, is exactly where I'm meant to be.

I take a deep breath and feel the warmth in the air. I know in my heart that my journey in this life is coming to an end soon. I don't want it to, but I know it's something I can no longer escape from. Almost three years of this painful, yet beautiful, journey have passed. I'm scared, but somehow, I feel at peace. I have built a foundation of love, of strength, between myself and my family, something so incredible that, even in my absence, the love I've created will live on. My grandson, Leo always says to me "Come on Grandpa, you can make it!" And those words have never seemed so clear to me as they are now. In that moment, I realise, I have made it.

THE MORE SAND HAS ESCAPED FROM THE HOURGLASS OF OUR LIFE, THE CLEARER WE SHOULD SEE THROUGH IT

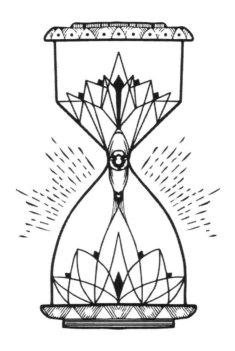

NICCOLO MACHIAVELLI

CHAPTER ONE

It's bright and early on a Saturday morning. The sun is beaming down onto my newest venture, Heart Kitchen. I love food and when I say love, I mean I completely find food the most amazing, beautiful thing in the whole entire world. Food is a huge passion of mine. I grew up surrounded by strong, influential women teaching me their secret recipes in the kitchen. I used to stand mesmerized watching my granny with utter fascination. Even her fresh fried egg sandwich, on beautiful fluffy just-baked bread, with ice-cold butter, used to get my taste buds excited!

I trained as a chef in my teens, but was kicked out of college for not taking it all seriously enough. Looking back on that now, it's not a regret, as it's all led me to the path I ended up on and I've enjoyed every second. I filled most of my adult years with building my business in plant hire and building a future for our family with my beautiful wife, Sue. She raised our four incredible children, Phoebe, Murray, Niamh and Robson, all of whom I'm so proud, while I worked hard towards our dreams as a family and here we are now.

Our family home, Keepers Cottage, is surrounded by ancient woodland, miles from any bustle from the rest of the world. It's just perfect. Here is where I began my newest creation, Heart Kitchen. Situated within an outbuilding at Keepers, an old converted stable with beautiful beams and slate floors, overlooking fields and apple orchards, just beautiful! It's here I created and pulled together a vision I'd held so clear for many years, a cookery school, but not just any cookery school. This was something totally new, a completely different experience from your average cookery school. This difference was something I feel so passionately about, and that is…cooking from the heart.

Your heart is powerful. It's an incredible place to work from, especially when working with food. It makes you feel the process of the dish you're creating. It makes you feel gratitude towards all the food that's been offered to you. You feel in absolute awe of the universe and what it's provided for you. It's amazing. Furthermore, this way of cooking also has immense power when bringing people together. A group of people cooking with me may start the day not knowing much about one another, maybe feeling anxious, maybe uncertain, but by the time we've finished, they are wrapped in a blissful bubble of love, surrounded by an ambience of gratitude for what they've created together that day and gratitude for one another. It really is magical.

I always look at that building with pride, feeling so lucky my journey has guided me this way to something I love so much. I'm so fortunate, so blessed, this has always been a dream of mine and my sense of purpose has been fulfilled by living this dream. It's just epic! I stand for a moment looking, noticing, taking it all in and memories come to me of my most recent cookery day at Heart Kitchen; a day that holds a firm place within my heart; a day in the Italian Heart Kitchen.

"Right guys, welcome to you all. I'm so excited to have you here today in this beautiful space, sharing this experience. It's just great to have you here! So, I want you to stand here for a moment. I want you to take a long deep breath, just inhale a really slow, deep breath right to the bottom of your lungs. Look at the food around you on this table. Look at everything there and take it all in, breathe it all in. I want you to feel absolute gratitude for it. Think how it's grown, how it's sacrificed itself to be on our table today. Think about all the beautiful sunshine it's absorbed to nourish itself, all the fresh rain and rich soil. Feel the power of the food, how does it make you feel? Do you feel happy? Do you feel excited? Maybe you're nervous. Let those feelings come, acknowledge them, it's all good... I want you to pick up that onion. I want you to thank it. I want you to love it! Go on, pick it up! Thank it for everything, guys; for working with you today; for offering itself; for being beautifully delicious. Just thank it."

This particular day was being held by myself and my fellow foodie and dear friend Celia. We founded Heart Kitchen together, along with Sue. Cooking with Celia, sharing these experiences with her filled every part of me with deep joy. It's a real precious thing when you find "your people", people that vibrate at the same frequency as you, you just totally get one another, it's wonderful. We spend a lot of time, the three of us, often foraging in the woodlands and shopping at local food markets for the freshest produce. Sue also has her allotment where she grows anything she can. We use all her harvest for our cookery days at Heart Kitchen, using ingredients that are in season, it's brilliant. Although not everything seemed to blossom in the way she'd hoped. Ask her about the caterpillar roast dinner we once ended up with!

The day was made up of mainly friends and family, but also extra special as my dear friend Alessandro had flown over from Italy with his two Italian Nonnas to join us, so it was even more of an authentic Italian experience. Sue and two of our children were there as well. I always like to start the day as crazy as I can. I want everyone to feel the excitement I feel when I cook. I want them to feel that same passion. Sue is, luckily, slightly calmer than me when it comes to my cookery classes. She is the gift that grounds me and that reminder to me that I should "rein it in". Not that I ever really listen. We always start each day checking in with one another, in one big group, letting what feelings flow, flow. It's an important part for me, standing together, being present in that moment, something we don't do enough as human beings. Just taking a deep breath, letting it all move, and looking at the day we are about to start with a grateful open heart.

That day, I set everyone the task of making the most delicious Italian ragu. I wanted them to make their own fresh pasta, prepare their own delicious soffritto and sauces and bring it all together into one beautifully tasty dish to enjoy and share around the table at the end of the day!

Some of you reading this now may already know how much I have always loved Italy. I have such a magnetic feeling to all things Italian. I love to travel there, I love the food, I love the people. I even bought myself a little Italian Vespa, which could be seen as a mid-life crisis purchase but I assure you it wasn't! I then followed that with a camper van, which I called Giuseppe, why not I say! I sometimes wonder if, in a past life, I lived as an Italian farmer. With a deep brown tan, wrinkles on my weathered face that showed my life's journey, tales of days in the blissful sunshine. Hands that were hard from the work and love I had put into growing all sorts of wonderful things in my fields and orchards; hands that were stained with the soil; hands that told a story.

We spent the whole day preparing the most delicious feast, with everyone taking so much pride in the art of cooking. We laughed, we even cried, connecting on so many deep levels over something so very simple, food.

At the end of the day with the sun slowly setting across the fields we sat in the Heart Kitchen, around the big oak table, with full plates of delicious food, glasses of Italian wine, feeling such pride in what we had created together as a group. Beautiful fresh pasta, amazing flavourful ragu. The whole room was filled with an abundance of love. The conversations between people were ones with depth, meaning and love. I knew my work was done for that day. I had set the intention of inspiring them all with the gift of food and I had done exactly that.

COOKING IS LIKE LOVE. IT SHOULD BE ENTERED INTO WITH ABANDON OR NOT AT ALL

JULIA CHILD

CHAPTER TWO

Have you ever had a "wow" moment? A moment where you sit there and think to yourself, *'Wow, just wow'*? This is the way I felt when my first grandson arrived in the world. It was a chilly morning in February 2016. My daughter, Phoebe, had been in labour all night. Sue and I barely slept, mainly with excitement, but we also had that parental protection instinct, hoping Phoebe was OK and hoping that everything would go as smoothly as possible for her and her husband, Chris. We already had the gift of three beautiful Step-Grandchildren, Summer, Scarlett and Logan, but to have Phoebe, our eldest daughter bringing a new life into the world was amazing. It's actually rather unnerving, knowing someone you love so dearly is experiencing great pain. However, it's with hope and trust that something beautiful will be there at the end. Funny feeling, that nervousness.

I remember when Phoebe announced her pregnancy. I felt a bit shocked to say the least. I thought to myself "I'm too young to be a grandparent" and I was always a worrier. I wanted my daughter, Phoebe, to have everything in the world, as I did for all four of my children. I didn't want her to miss any opportunities or miss out on her younger years. As my wife reminded me, "Simon, she's not actually young. She's a woman now. This was always the next step for Phoebe and it's an amazing step".

Over the months, as I watched her belly grow, I could

feel my own excitement grow. By the time she was due to have the baby, I was like a child at Christmas. I couldn't contain it. I had all the feelings, had all the butterflies. I was overjoyed to start this new chapter in all of our lives. The next generation of our family being born into the world.

When Phoebe was approaching the end of her pregnancy in December 2015, I was diagnosed with cancer. This came as a bit of a shocker for me as I always saw myself as invincible, *Super-Hero-Si*. I had a humungous passion for life. I was at the height of my career. I'd succeeded with my companies and I was finally living out my true passion with Heart Kitchen. To say I was stunned is an understatement. I just don't think I, or anyone I knew, saw this coming.

When I heard the words 'terminal cancer', I thought to myself, *"Well, there's absolutely no way I am taking that."* I had so much to live for right now, so much to stay on planet Earth for, so much to share with others. Sue and I had so many adventures around the world planned. We'd spent the last thirty years building an amazing life for our children and ourselves and now they were all grown up, it was **our** time. Time for us to spend with one another; time to explore this fascinating world and all it has to offer together. As I liked to say in jest to my kids, "time to squander some of my hard-earned wealth!"

When I was first diagnosed, my immediate thoughts were of our new grandchild. If there was a reason to stay, then I knew right now that the reason was him. I had to stay for him. There was no way in the world I wasn't sticking around for his big arrival! I had so much I wanted to share with him, so much I wanted to teach him. I wanted to be the one to show him how truly beautiful this world is and all it has to offer. I knew deep in my heart that was something I had to stay for. I felt blessed for the gift in this, that the universe had given our family something so precious at this exact time, something that would shift our focus from the negative of cancer and move it to the positive of a brand-new life. What a gift!

My grandson arrived and wow, just WOW! Leo, my little Leo. I can't explain that feeling, unless you're a grandparent yourself, then you'll know. But that feeling of complete joy; that feeling of utter bliss; you feel so much love and so much gratitude. That, for me, was a "WOW" moment.

My darling Leo, holding you in my arms, I took in every detail of you. Cradling you so lovingly, I knew little about you but I could feel so much, your curiosity, the wisdom behind your little blue eyes, the calmness, the love. I didn't understand why, but something inside told me we'd met before and the connection to you, my grandson, that we would share from now on, would be something inexplicable. Something that cannot be defined by science or explanation. Just a magic. A special type of magic where two souls meet once again in a brand-new chapter and my gosh, how incredible that is.

"My darling little Leo, I'll call him my Lion Boy!" I said to Phoebe, "My little Leo Lion. What adventures can we get up to, hey, whilst we still have time?"

AND SUDDENLY YOU KNOW: IT'S TIME TO START SOMETHING NEW AND TRUST THE MAGIC OF BEGINNINGS

MEISTER ECKHART

CHAPTER THREE

The day I told my family I was ill was an extremely hard one. I was given my diagnosis on Christmas Eve, but Sue and I chose not to announce it until after Christmas Day, as we didn't want to ruin the festivities. We just wanted to enjoy every part of it. This happening to me made me realise it could be my last Christmas and I didn't want to spend it being sad. I wanted to embrace every moment.

The thing is we often see our path as so steady, so clear. When in reality it's nothing like that. Life is full of ups and downs, twists and turns. It throws curve balls at us and we have a choice whether to embrace those and do our best or crumble under the strain of it all and crumbling was not an option to me.
Our other daughter, Niamh, was in Canada at the time. She works as a snowboard instructor, so is always somewhere else in the world, living it up in the minuses, creating and living her dream! Super proud of her for that. I remember being asked to describe all of my four children by a friend and which quality of mine I thought they had. My responses were… Murray has my business-like mind and practical side, Robson has my fire and that passion I hold deep inside, Niamh has my sense of adventure, the willingness to learn and Phoebe, well what does Phoebe have? Hmmmmm, I'd say Phoebe is more like Sue, simply just really needy. I chuckle to myself now remembering Phoebe's reaction, one of complete dramatized shock. She was always the easiest to wind up out of the four of them.

On Boxing Day 2015, we sat around our big oak table at Keepers Cottage, and I shared the news of my cancer. I'd been having tests for a month or so, so everyone was awaiting some type of answer, but I don't think they ever in a million years expected it to be this. There was a sense of uncertainty in the room and deep sadness. The boys were very much on edge, not wanting to sit down, not knowing how to be, how to feel. Phoebe sat with Sue, sobbing whilst cradling her pregnant belly, with complete heartache at the reality we were now facing. Niamh was on Skype, just sat in complete shock. It was about 2am in Canada, but it was important we told them all together. I don't remember much about when we spoke. It's all a blur, apart from one moment when I declared my full intentions starting this new journey. "I don't want you to worry, guys. I don't want this to consume you as I'm not letting it consume me. We shouldn't project anger onto my cancer. If we do that, we are only making it stronger. It will feed off our negativity. I want us to love it and feed it only good stuff. I don't know how this will end, or how this will plan out, but I'm going to give it all I've got. So, look at me now and hear this, I am NOT going anywhere right now. This isn't the end, I promise you that!"

Don't get me wrong, there was fear and anger inside me, so much anger, but I made a choice. I could sit there, hating my cancer, feeling furious, doing what many people do and questioning over and over "why me?" Was it bad karma for my mistakes? If so, it was absolutely brutal karma, but fair play! I could have wasted endless days feeling miserable, feeling defeated but I didn't want to do that. I wanted, with whatever time I had left, however long that may be, to live. I chose to live. I spent so much time wondering, feeling, thinking, tracking and all I could conclude is this; you are exactly where you are meant to be. Trust in your journey. The universe has the plans. Just go with it, embrace, evolve, enjoy.

My health, by the time Leo was born in February, had started to go pretty much downhill. My liver wasn't playing ball and I had a rather off-putting yellow hue to my skin. I had met with my medical team, who to this day I feel so blessed to have had - my oncologists, Justin and Dan, my surgeon, Kito Fusai, and my dietician, Jane. I was under their care and they were willing to try anything they could to prolong the time I had left. I always referred to my surgeon, Kito, as a surgical wizard. Kito was up for trying anything. He had a box of tricks and wasn't going to miss one. My first oncologist, Justin, was almost as 'out there' as myself. Upon meeting him, his first question to me was "Simon, if you could be any Harry Potter character, then who would you be?" I knew right then that this oncologist was the one to help me if anyone could. When you put a bunch of people together that are as 'out there' as I am…. magic happens! I was lucky with the gift I had been given, with the team and support network I had around me. I felt in safe hands. I felt as if together, we'd explore all options and I was open to anything and everything. As I said already, I chose life.

Our journey in life is a gift we often take for granted. We can't help it, it's almost programmed in us to look at what we don't have, look at what's wrong in our lives, focus on what's missing, but doing that does us no favours, we only end up increasingly negative and unhappier. What if I told you it's as simple as noticing the positives, noticing the gifts, it really is that simple. Our lives are full with an abundance of gifts, we just need to take time to notice them. This is a choice I now have to consciously make every day; otherwise where does that leave me? I'll tell you where, it leaves me in the drama of cancer, the chaos, the sadness and what good would that do to my body when it's already challenged with something else. To feel strong, to have the drive to see this path out until the very end, I must approach everything with an open heart, whatever the path may be, wherever it may lead me. Gratitude first and always.

I AM LEARNING TO TRUST THE JOURNEY, EVEN WHEN I DON'T UNDERSTAND IT

MILA BRON

CHAPTER FOUR

I sat a little longer peacefully with my new grandson in my arms. Again, I'll tell you, the love I felt was out of this world. He felt like such a gift to me. He'd arrived at the exact time that I needed him. The time when, not that I'd let on to anyone, I was feeling weak. I was noticing changes in my body, my energy levels were low, I struggled to do simple daily things that I'd done for years without needing a three-hour nap afterwards. I had shorter patience, which I'm guessing was due to the frustration of what I was going through. The chemo made me snappier too. I actually didn't like myself too much when going through chemo. I felt totally different. I struggled to find my joy or my passions, but Leo's arrival gave me a new feeling, something I'd not had before.

I had not always been such a positive person. Like many of you, I've had some real low points. I struggled for many years with the acceptance of love. When I was two years old, my father left me, my sister and my mother. It's a time I don't remember clearly, nor do I remember any specific moments. However, it's a time for me that I felt pain about and I did for many years. I let that pain consume me at times, I let it control a lot in my life. And to be honest with you, I wasn't even aware of that until I started a process working alongside someone who helped me to heal those "damaged" parts myself by opening everything up, exposing it all and dealing with it. With all challenges in life I truly believe if we dig deep, and allow ourselves to feel them fully, great healing can be received, and that is so important in living a balanced, fulfilling and peaceful life. We must allow the time needed to heal only then can we move forward. I'm thankful for this teaching in my life, as it enabled me to move forward, to embrace life. Until then, I'd never really looked at my life and seen how truly and deeply blessed I was. I had an amazing wife, who had raised our four children whilst I could go and work and provide. I had a beautiful home. I had incredible friends and family. I was surrounded by an abundance of love and knowing this allowed me to become who I am. It allowed me to enjoy life, love life and cherish life.

My wife, my living, breathing angel, was the one who encouraged me to seek this healing help. If it wasn't for her, I'm not sure my journey with cancer would be as it was. I wouldn't have had the capability to connect with how I was feeling. With this ability I felt powerful. I knew who I was, I knew what my body needed, I was ready to take it all on and I did.

A few months passed, which were filled with many visits from Leo. He was growing rapidly and changing by the minute! He recognised me now, he'd giggle, he'd smile, it was wonderful and filled my heart with a wealth of joy. I had trips into London for my chemo with my oncologist, Justin, and Skype calls with my dietician, Jane, who was absolutely amazing, strict, but amazing nevertheless. I had to cut out two of my favourite things for a while in order to help my body - coffee and sugar, can you imagine? The two main fuels that I had used daily to keep myself going for years. Obviously, they hadn't done such a great job at the "going" part, in hindsight.

By this time, I had taken big steps away from all my businesses. Heart Kitchen had shut up shop for now which broke my heart, however it was necessary as I couldn't commit to running any cookery schools with my health being so unpredictable. My plant hire company, I handed over to my sons, Muz and Rob and to my most trusted friend, Vinnie. Now wasn't a time I could go in and give anything of myself to people at work, so it was all necessary. Sue and I discussed possibly moving house. Keepers Cottage had been our family home for over fifteen years, but now felt time to downsize, to move into something right for me and Sue. I didn't have the energy to take care of all the land and woodland and it wouldn't have been fair to Sue either, if I passed sooner than we thought, to be left with the huge task of organising a house move and setting down new roots. So, we looked into some ideas and made some new plans. Again, this was something I didn't ever think we'd have to do; as I said, our future plans consisted of travelling the world, taking time for ourselves, but life, as it does, had other plans.

TRUE HEALING OCCURS WHEN I GIVE MYSELF PERMISSION TO FEEL WHATEVER FEELINGS LIVE BELOW THE TRIGGERS

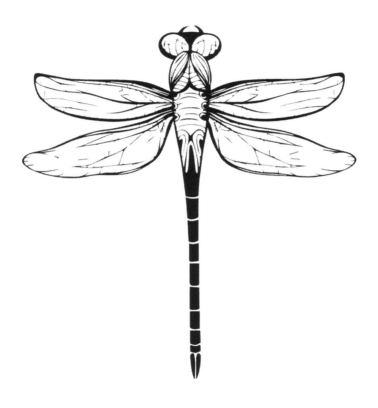

GABBY BERNSTEIN

CHAPTER FIVE

So, after a few months of more chemo, more strict diets and scans I was going to be having a major operation I urgently needed. My liver wasn't playing ball and I was starting to resemble the shade of a banana with my skin yellowing more and more each day. My surgeon Kito, was hoping to remove some of the cancer in my pancreas and stomach along with sorting out my liver issue. The procedure was called Whipples. He was basically going in and chopping loads of parts away from me. It's pretty gruesome actually. Technically, if it all went to plan, I would come home half the man I was (in terms of my organs!)

My family and I had been building up to the day, a day I'd been absolutely dreading. It was now only 24 hours away, and I was feeling overly anxious. Right now, was the time I needed to feel strong and I didn't, in fact, I felt quite the opposite. I felt extremely vulnerable, like a small child, filled with nerves, anxiety and fear. I knew this operation needed to happen, life would most likely be a hell of a lot shorter without it, but I was uncomfortable with this feeling. I could only do one thing and that was to remind myself repeatedly of how strong I am, how far I'd come and how much more of my journey I had left to live.

I had managed to block out the dawning of this day by occupying myself with distractions; dinners out (when I had the energy); little trips down to Brighton, one of my favourite places (to be fair, anywhere by the sea suits me); time with family; trips out with Leo. But there was no escape. It was something that had to be done, so I guessed I should just put on my big-boy pants and get on with it. It's completely out of my control after all. In my surgical team, I have total trust.

…………..

I woke up in ICU, in The Wellington hospital, in London. I saw the machines beeping and flashing, myriad wires all over my body, tubes in my nose. My body hurt. My head felt foggy. There were nurses by my bedside smiling, stroking my hand to comfort me saying "It's OK, Simon". Sue was on the other side, asleep, her head resting on my bed, holding my hand. I imagine she'd been there all night, not that I was even aware of the time of day right now. She looked peaceful, calm. I always loved to watch her sleep. Before I became ill, I used to make sure every morning I'd wake up early and get her a cup of tea ready, taking it up to our room for her to sip on as she woke. I'd often shout to her "Beary, wake up, come and see this sunrise!" She wasn't much of an early riser nowadays. I always believed she was making up for many years of lost sleep after raising our four children. At Keepers Cottage, we'd see the most incredible sunrises over the fields. The sun would be all shades of orange, yellow and ethereal white. It would appear over the tops of the trees, above our woodland. I always felt so blessed waking up in the mornings, looking out and seeing the beautiful sunrise with Sue. I'd hold her in my arms. We'd be so peaceful. We'd be so happy.

"Hey, darling, you're awake!" Sue said from my bedside, "How are you feeling?" How was I feeling? I didn't really have the words to respond. I felt terrified. I felt pain. I felt sadness but I also felt safe. I felt loved. I felt calm. Impossible to know how you can feel so many emotions in one moment, but I guess things like this have that effect.

My voice was too weak to respond, so I smiled at Sue to let her know I was OK. Little tears rolled down her cheeks. I could feel her sadness. "I love you, my darling," she said. I would have done anything in that moment to jump up and hold her tight in my arms and make it all OK for her, but I couldn't right now. She and I both knew my body was too weak. I fell back into a deep sleep.

I could only guess how many minutes, hours and days passed when I was in the ICU. There were a few issues with my recovery, hence me spending so many days there. I was aware of voices when people visited, but not awake enough to be able to respond. I knew when my kids where there. I was often aware of the noises from my many machines, lots of beeping and people rushing in when a few beeped at once. I heard my mum a lot. She would never say much when I was at my weakest in hospital. She'd just sit calmly, holding my hand tight. I'd hear her quietly sob next to me. It was hard for Mum as I had always been her pillar. I'd made sure that she was well looked after, as she deserved to be. She raised me and my sister single-handedly until she met my stepdad and I always vowed to myself that I wouldn't let her struggle. I wanted to be able to look after her as she had done for me. For my mum, I knew this was beyond tough. Let's face it, nobody should have to watch their child suffer, no matter how grown up they may be. It's a heart-breaking thing for a parent.

I lay in the ICU, still in and out of consciousness. I'd drift off and be with Leo. He would show up a lot for me in my dreams when I was poorly. Often, at times when I felt weak, when I was considering giving up, I'd see him there and know I must stay. He would appear with no words exchanged between us, simply a feeling. I would feel the fullness of his love and know that I had to be there for him. It gave me so much strength seeing him in my dreams.

I woke a few days later to the wizard himself, Mr Kito Fusai, standing by my bedside. He was an Italian man with a smooth Italian accent and always dressed in the most immaculate Italian suits, with long silver hair that I was rather jealous of. *How did it look so silky?* I'd think to myself.

"Simon, how are you feeling?" he asked while holding my hand. He was so kind-natured. He understood so much about me, about my journey with cancer, about how important my family were and how much I wanted to be better to enjoy life to its fullest, to travel with Sue, to go on adventures with my new grandson.

I winced and chuckled at him. "Well, to be honest, I've felt better and on a scale of one to ten, then hmmm, let me think how to describe it. I know, it hurts like fuck!"

Mr Fusai laughed at me, "Simon, Simon, you have such a way with words, a nine or ten would have sufficed." We had great banter between us, always laughing and joking. We also shared a similar passion for travel and food. He told me of a place I'd never heard of much called Formentera, in the Balearic Islands. He said "Simon, when you are home and a little stronger, you must travel. You need the ocean, you need some sunshine, you must go there and heal for a little while." I thought to myself, *yes*, I couldn't have agreed more. The sea was calling me, the sun was calling me, I needed to rest, I needed to recoup, I needed to heal. And that's exactly what I did.

YOU NEVER KNOWN HOW STRONG YOU ARE UNTIL BEING STRONG IS THE ONLY CHOICE YOU HAVE

CAYLA MILLS

CHAPTER SIX

Staring out into the vast, wide ocean, I knew my surgeon had been right; I needed rest, I needed to be here, on this beautiful beach, with my darling Sue. Recovering, recuperating and reconnecting. I'd always been such a busy bee, I could never sit still, so this was good for me. The warmth of the sun on my skin, the sweet smell of salty air, brought me right back to myself, away from any stress or worry. I felt whole and balanced again.

Have you ever sat still? I mean, not just still in yourself, I mean still in your mind, still in your thoughts, still with your breath. I mean, wow, the feelings you have in that moment, the gratitude you feel, the peace you feel, it's mind blowing. It's so important to do. I had never done it in all my years until recently. It was necessary for me now, not only physically, as my body was weakening further, but for my own mind, my own self. I think to myself, really, in life, what is so bad? Yes, I'm ill and yes, I'm not my "healthy self" any more, but rather than focusing on what I am not or what I do not have, how about thinking about what I *do* have, what I *am* now, how incredible life actually is *right now*. Life is amazing, it really is. I once read a quote that said, *"We live on a blue planet that circles around a ball of fire next to a moon that moves the sea, yet we don't believe in miracles?"* Doesn't that give you an insane perspective on how incredible life is? Breathe, be still, calm your thoughts, calm the mind…. do it now. Put this book down, close your eyes, take some deep breaths and embrace that overwhelming, amazing, energetic bomb of gratitude.

When you sit in stillness, you notice so much. You become aware of so much. This is all so important within our human existence; we must take time to allow for some stillness. I started to see, more and more, how much could change in a moment when doing this.

Formentera was amazing. For anyone who has never been, go. My top destinations would be there, Bali, Es Vedra in Ibiza and probably the whole of Italy! I loved exploring culture. I loved seeing what treasures the world had to offer in all corners of the world and above all I loved seeing it with my soulmate, Sue. To be with her, by the ocean, absorbing the beautiful sea air and blissful sunshine was what fed my soul. It filled my heart with joy, it gave me time to reflect, time to refocus, time that was so necessary to heal. We are so busy in our lives, so many days filled with jobs, to-do lists, that we never allow ourselves that time to regenerate. We must, *you* must. You deserve it, your body deserves it. We must slow down and let ourselves heal.

When we returned from our trip, we were greeted by a house full! Phoebe, Chris and Leo were there along with my other kids; Muz, Niamh and Rob and the boys' partners, Lisa and Jodie. We didn't even know that Niamh was coming home, but she'd always chuck a surprise in here and there! It meant so much to feel so supported by them all. All of my life, I had been the protector, the one helping them. Don't get me wrong, I still am and will always be that, but now they had really shown me how incredibly amazing each of them was by fully giving themselves to me and to Sue, to support us on this journey.

I fell into Niamh's arms. To see her overflows my heart with so much joy. I think, because I can't see Niamh so often with her travelling, it's just incredibly special for me when I do get to be with her. Tears streamed down both of our faces as we squeezed one another tight. When she's away, I always feel I'm missing something. I am immensely proud of her for her choice in life, travelling the world and teaching snowboarding, but boy, do I miss her when she goes away. When she was born, Sue was poorly after labour and went into emergency theatre, leaving me alone with Niamh, this tiny little girl, only minutes old. I remember looking at her beautiful face, feeling so blessed to be holding her in my arms, feeling so excited to introduce her to her older brother and sister, but I also felt scared. Sue was rushed away so quickly into theatre and the thought of something being seriously wrong and something terrible happening to her tore my heart into pieces. After all, to me, what was the world without Sue in it? She was my rock; she held us all together. Sue is, and will always be, my angel.

"Lion boy! Grandpa has returned!!!" Leo toddled over towards me. I felt so lucky to have Leo. We all did. I felt so blessed to know how much he is loved. It gave me reassurance that when the time came when I wouldn't be here, he would still be surrounded by amazingly strong people who loved him unconditionally. He was the most precious gift to our family, one whose impact we could have never truly understood or appreciated until he arrived. He was my motivation, a new reason for living, I adored him and he adored me.

I had never imagined the impact Leo would have on me. Yes, I had my own children and had been lucky enough to have that experience, but I had never really taken time before Leo arrived to deeply think about how my life would change. Children are such a gift, they come to this world with such light. To be in his company, even if only for a moment, would lift my spirit. Such a huge blessing, such an immense gift.

JUST ONE SMALL POSITIVE THOUGHT IN THE MORNING CAN CHANGE YOUR WHOLE DAY

DALAI LAMA

CHAPTER SEVEN

Things were becoming very uncertain for me. I'd been back and forth to the hospital, had operations, chemo, I'd even had a scan and been told I was cancer-free at one point, but somehow, we always ended up back where we started, wrapped in the chaos that cancer creates. I knew there was so much more I needed to do on the planet. I didn't feel ready to just give up. My family would spend hours researching any other methods we could try, any other options. We didn't want to leave any stone unturned. I wanted to be with Leo. I wanted to watch him grow. I wanted to be here for him and the grandchildren that I hadn't yet had, to teach and cherish them all. That was important to me. I had so much unfinished business. So many reasons to stay and such a great longing to stay.

Several more months of ups and downs went by, with trips to hospital, test after test and of course that god-awful chemo. I'd continued to stick to the strict diet, no sugar and no caffeine, except on an occasional treat day where I'd sit in the sunshine, in my favourite Italian cafe in Marlow, Satollo. I'd sip on the freshest, most beautiful cup of Italian coffee and treat myself to a slice of boiled orange cake or delicious carrot cake. I know I shouldn't but to fully deny myself those two indulgences is something I chose not to do. I'd often take Leo with me. He was a big baby chino fan - a genius invention. No more sharing your cappuccino froth, kids can have their very own baby chino. Epic!

We would often spend lazy afternoons sitting outside the café on their red and white stripped deck chairs. Leo would always ask for a balloon from the party shop next door and, of course, I could never say no. So, he'd play in the courtyard with his big red balloon, while Sue, Phoebe and I would enjoy freshly made cakes and beautiful coffee in each other's company. What a gift to just sit outside a coffee shop and watch the world go by. It's actually one of my favourite things to do. To see people go about their daily life and see their faces, some with looks of joy, some with worry. It brings me back to myself and helps me notice and appreciate the simple joys in my own life.

We'd now moved to Marlow, something I had wanted to do for a long time. Keepers Cottage had been the best family home for us all, but all the children had grown up now and it just wasn't right for us anymore. Even though it was sad to say goodbye, I knew the next chapter for Sue and I was on the horizon which filled me with excitement. We found our final project home, which we planned to renovate; that was extremely exciting, something else to work towards. We bit the bullet, bought the project house and moved into a rented home while we threw ourselves into the renovations. Marlow also worked well for me in regards to my health. Everything was just a short walk away, the supermarkets, the coffee shops, the doctors. I made great friends with a lot of the locals in the shops, one of my favourites was the Butcher's Tap, an absolutely fantastic butcher. As they prepared your beautifully freshly cut steaks, you could sit with a scotch egg or pie while you waited. I often went there with some of my dearest friends - what better than a pie and a catch up in the Butcher's?!

During this time, my health got a little worse. My body was running on empty; I'd started having seizures, so I was unable to drive anymore, which was incredibly frustrating and quite honestly made me feel degraded in every sense. I never used to let Sue or the kids drive me, but I found, yet again, I was having to swallow my pride and let others help me now.

I often got temperature spikes, picking up any bug going around. It was a real struggle to feel "healthy". I found myself having to give things a miss, such as parties, Leo's nursery Christmas concert. Actually, even Christmas was hard. I'd have to sneak off for naps to try and rebuild my energy just to be able to partake in the day itself. I can't stress to you how busy a person I used to be. I was the man holding the parties, the dad doing all I could for everyone. I was busy all the time, so I found this new way of life unimaginably hard.

When I got temperature spikes, I'd often spend days in bed, in and out of hot, sweaty, deep sleeps. The pain I'd feel in my body, the confusion in my mind was torture. Each time, I'd never know, *was this the last time? Is this how the end feels? Surely, I can beat this.* I'd often have vivid deep dreams. I've never been one for remembering much of my dreams, but at that time, I had a dream I couldn't forget, one that played on mind for days, weeks, months after. I was unwell at home after a chemotherapy session. I'd gone to bed with a very high temperature after battling with Sue that there was no way I would go to hospital tonight, regardless of my temperature. Sue was a stickler for the rules and she worried so much, understandably, but the last place I ever wanted to be after sizzling my organs with toxic chemotherapy all day was a hospital bed. We'd have the same battle every time.

"We're going into hospital, Simon!"
"I'm not going in!"
"You're being ridiculous, Si."
"It's my life and I'll do what I like."

I was acting like a rebellious teenager and in hindsight, the most sensible thing for anyone who may be in my situation is…. just go to hospital. Stop being so bloody stubborn and accept the help and care you need at that moment in time. I clearly struggled to get my head around this, so take that on board now, if you're in a similar situation to me.

So, I'd gone up to bed, temperature sky high, and fallen into a dazed, strange sleep. My body hurt all over. I had so much pain around my stomach and my back, it was as if I could feel the poison of the chemo shooting through every vein, every muscle, every nerve, trying to destroy anything it didn't like in its path. I'd fallen into a fretful sleep, I am dreaming, but I'm still so aware of the heat coming off my skin, aware of the agony I'm in, when at the foot of my bed appears a man.

He has a bright white and gold glow around his whole

body. His energy is calm, it's peaceful. I don't feel scared at all, in fact he feels familiar, safe, almost as though I know him. I realise he looks to me like someone I've been drawn towards a lot lately, St Francis of Assisi. I admire the work he did, his Camino, the walking route across Italy; For those who don't know about the Camino, it's official name is "The Way of St Francis" The walk consists of a 28-day trek beginning in Florence, walking through Tuscany, onto Umbria and Assisi and ending in Rome at the Vatican. The walk is inspired by his life, when he himself took and ancient road from Florence to Rome and walked the 550-kilometre journey. I often read the words of his prayer and use them as a reminder to be grateful every day....

So, at the foot of my bed stands St Francis. He speaks to me and asks me if I'm ready. I feel confused, ready for what? To die? Don't get me wrong, I knew my time was borrowed at the moment, but I wasn't expecting a call from the pearly gates so soon. I look back and say nothing. He then looks over to the side of my bed and smiles. I look too and I see my family all standing together by my bed, Sue, Phoebe, Murray, Niamh and Robson. They all seem sad. Sad, as if I'm not there anymore. They're standing together, arms draped around one another, there's a feeling of heartache, of deep sadness. The boys are supporting and holding their mum and sisters but looking down to the floor. Sue and the girls are sobbing, tears rolling down their faces. Then a child parts a way through between Sue and Phoebe, it's Leo. He's older in this image, around three years old. He walks towards me,

49

comes up to the side of my bed, calmly and peacefully takes my hand. He says no words, just holds my hand and looks up at me with love in his eyes. I look towards the end of my bed and see who I feel is St Francis walking away, towards the same glow that surrounded him. At that point I don't know in which direction to go - to follow the beautiful glow or to stay holding my grandson's hand. I then feel a massive overwhelming sense that I am being given a choice, to stay or to go. I look at Leo and I smile and hold his hand tightly and then…. I wake.

I often sit and think about this dream as it had such a huge impact on me. Not only seeing my family that way but then seeing Leo trying to lead me back to them. That was a recurring reminder. They are my reason to stay. I must stay.

START BY DOING WHAT'S NECESSARY; THEN DO WHAT'S POSSIBLE; AND SUDDENLY YOU ARE DOING THE IMPOSSIBLE

FRANCIS OF ASSISI

CHAPTER EIGHT

Leo was growing up fast. It was the summer of 2018, he was two now and becoming quite the character. He would absolutely overwhelm me with his eager attitude to learn so much about life. He was always running from one place to the next, totally immersed in whatever he was being shown, permanently curious about everything. If I was doing something, he would need to come and join in. If I was eating something, he would sit with me and eat it too. If I was poorly and having a day where I struggled, he would sit calmly next to me, giving me cuddles of comfort and little words of reassurance. He just felt so familiar to me. I felt so safe in his presence. We just knew one another's souls so well. And the joy, oh the joy, he gave me so much joy.

I took him to Ibiza (another incredibly beautiful island), on a holiday that, deep down, I knew was my last, not that I would share that with anyone at the time. We went for a week, Leo, Sue, Niamh, Phoebe and Robson's partner, Jodie. Phoebe was pregnant with her second little boy, which made it even more exciting. We had so much fun exploring together. We raced across the beach, built sandcastles, we ate every ice-cream option possible, we bought an inflatable boat and sailed out to sea and shared precious moments as we watched the sunset across the sea every evening, cuddled up on a blanket on the sand. The world felt like our oyster and in Leo's presence, I felt strong, powerful. I had a reason to embrace life, to enjoy it and I did. Funny, I never fully and totally accepted at the time that this would be my final trip, my last holiday. I had many more adventures planned and many more things I wanted to tick off my bucket list, but how perfect, how incredibly special, that the last place I travelled to was hand in hand with my darling Leo and side by side with my girls. What a precious memory for us all to treasure for the rest of our lives. What a moment to have shared.

More time had passed. My family and I had been lucky enough to share so many experiences and moments. I'd got to walk Phoebe down the aisle to marry her husband Chris, which was a moment both of us will cherish forever. My son, Murray, also married his fiancée Lisa, a day I was just so incredibly proud to be part of. It was wonderful to see so many of the people I adore, wonderful to witness so much love, both weddings were just such magical, beautiful days, for which I feel deep gratitude, deep pride, and an abundance of love.

It was clear that the year of final moments was coming to an end. Time was running out, so to speak and I could feel it, I knew it deep down. I now needed a wheelchair as walking was just too hard for me. I'd also made the decision to not go into the hospital anymore, it wasn't something I could bring myself to do again. My body was weakening rapidly and I just wanted to make the most of the time I had left and I definitely didn't want to spend it stuck in hospital. I know, to some, that may have been seen as giving up, but for me, it wasn't that at all. It was quite simply, acceptance. Acceptance that my journey was coming to an end and with that said, asking myself "*what do I want to do*". So, instead of that I made the best decision for me and used that time I had left to embrace all I could with my family and friends. Time is so precious, I had to use it wisely.

The message felt clear - don't wait to do things you want to do. Don't wait for your kids to grow up to finally do things for your own happiness. Don't wait to experience life in all its beauty. You never know how much time you'll have. We are blessed with this life. Notice life, embrace it, use it well. Do all those things; please, do them for yourself and for your loved ones.

TIME HAS A WONDERFUL WAY OF
SHOWING US WHAT REALLY MATTERS

MARGARET PETERS

CHAPTER NINE

How crazy is it that in a small moment your entire life can be reshaped from how you once knew it? We wake up every day expecting the new day to be similar to yesterday. We pre-plan the day, the lists of jobs you'll do, the friends you'll meet, the meals you'll eat, but we never start the day thinking it could possibly be your last.

What would you do differently? Would you still rush around all day completing your never-ending list of jobs? Would you embrace those moments with a friend or loved one, knowing it was to be the last time you'd speak? Would you do those things you'd always wanted to do? What would you do?

By now, it was the winter of 2018 and I was on borrowed time from my doctor and my medical team. And so I began to organise things. I began with the sensible stuff, the organisation of "when I'm gone". I met with bank managers and solicitors. I talked with my sons about my business and the roles I now needed them to take on as the men of my family. I met old friends for breakfast in my town. I never let them know I was near the end. However, I'm sure that the time I said that goodbye to each of them, gave them that warm hug, saying "You take care of yourself," they knew. They knew, deep down, that it was goodbye. My body showed how poorly I was. I didn't resemble any part of myself any more. I was frail. I was weak. I looked and I felt as though I could break at any moment.

A precious memory was going to the Christmas lights switch on in Marlow. Me in my wheelchair, Leo in his buggy, both watching the big countdown to the lights illuminating the high street, the harmonious carols sung by local school children, the bustle and excitement of people for the festive season to begin. I treasure memories like this. These are moments of 'lasts', moments I know I won't get again, the last December, the last Christmas, the last months, the last days, the last minutes.

I was awaiting the arrival of my newest grandchild, Phoebe was due any day. I felt extremely poorly and spent most of my days sleeping. I found the very smallest of tasks exhausting. Inside, I still felt that fire and drive, but my body just didn't match up with that vibration anymore. It was giving up and I knew it. I managed to make it through and enjoy that Christmas, the Christmas of 2018, and to see in the new year with my family, with little Leo coming to wake me at midnight to tell me there were fireworks and to look outside at all the sparkly lights. We'd both had a little pre-New Year nap and Phoebe had promised me she'd wake us both so we could see 2019 in all together, one last time, just as I wanted it. We sat up together, cuddled up in bed under the duvet, just before the clock struck twelve, Leo with his cup of milk and me with a cup of tea, watching the fireworks together through the window, one last time, one last memory, for him and for me, just that one moment, what a gift, what a treasured memory. Leo, my lion, and Grandpa Simon, welcoming in 2019.

And so, the new year arrived, and with it, my new grandson, Gabriel. And what an angel he is. What a pure, calm soul he was. Unlike Leo, he didn't possess that fieriness I saw in myself. Instead, he gave me a different gift and that gift was comfort. Holding him, even so small, I felt calm. His energy was peaceful, his soul was new. He filled my whole being with peace, completion, fulfilment. I felt safe. I knew it would all be OK. He, like Leo, had arrived at the perfect time. Leo, my lion, gave me the reason to fight, to stay. Gabriel, my angel, gave me the peace to let go. Thank you. My two boys, for those gifts, thank you so much.

I made them both books full of pictures and memories - given their young ages, Leo about to turn three and Gabriel just a newborn, it felt important that they knew how loved they were and would always be. They had to know that wherever I was at the end of all this, the love still remained. It's where I'll remain, in their hearts. They were my gift. They both gave me more than I will ever get the chance to explain to them. Written in the pages of their books are my words to them, my wishes. Ones to be kept in their hearts forever.

My Wishes for You

Travel the world with passion and fire.

Peek under every stone (you never know what you
may find).

Love with all of your heart.

It's been tough to say goodbye, but as a family we've
learnt so much
about using all of our heart, being and strengths.

I'm sad that we didn't get more time together on this
planet, I know we would have had so much fun.

So, my darlings, wherever you are today, whatever
you're doing, know that my heart is fully with you.

Until we meet again,

Grandpa Simon
x

HOW LUCKY I AM TO HAVE SOMETHING
THAT MAKES SAYING GOODBYE SO HARD

A.A. MILNE

CHAPTER TEN

End of life care - these are words, as a family, we never wanted to hear. These are words that gave me a final destination. A destination I never wanted to go to. They are words of emptiness, words I can't quite attribute a proper emotion to. Words that lead to a confused feeling and overwhelming reality check of…how the hell did I end up here?

On one side, you have the pain, the utterly destroying, agonising pain of knowing your time is ending. Your time with loved ones, in this lifetime, has run its course. You'll no longer be walking the Earth as husband to your wife, brother to your sister, grandparent to your grandchild or father to your child. Instead, you'll part in a way you never wanted, completely out of anyone's control. You want to fight it, search for a solution, discover any possible way to stop this from happening, but you're not in control. You've never been in control, life will do as it's meant to do, to every single person. None of us has that control.

I started end of life care three weeks after Gabriel was born in January 2019. I became ill with a serious infection, drifting in and out of consciousness. Some things I remember; Sue trying to lift me off the sofa, I'm dripping in sweat, I'm hazed, I can't lift my body. She called our two sons in a panic, asking them to come right away, something wasn't right. I remember them arriving, both rushing over, their hands immediately pressing against my face. "Dad, Dad, come on Dad. What's going on? What's up?" The doctor was on the phone, asking Sue to make me comfortable in bed and he would be over right away. I remember being lifted and opening my eyes to see my eldest son, Murray, carrying me in his arms, as though I were a baby. I was so light, just bones clinging onto anything they could. He carried me to the bed, my arms wrapped around his neck. Setting me down, I looked up at him and murmured "I'm sorry, mate."

The doctor arrived and pronounced I had, in his words, "Three days. He has a maximum of three days. I'll make the necessary arrangements with the Rennie Grove nurses who will begin end the of life care treatment and make Simon comfortable. I suggest you call both your daughters and ask them to come immediately, along with any other family. Simon doesn't have long. I'm so sorry."

Funny, isn't it, how quickly things change? Moments before, you're enjoying making all those memories, despite knowing they're your last; they're still happening, you're still living, and then, it's as if time just stops, just stands still. Plans made for weeks ahead are cancelled; family are contacted and asked to prepare to say goodbye. It changes so quickly.

I knew this would be the outcome eventually, but somehow it still felt surreal to me. Three whole years of such determination almost felt lost, but I had to remind myself that it's not lost at all, nothing has been lost. Without that determination, that drive, that will to keep living, this would have ended much, much sooner. Yes, my body has slowly and gradually stopped coping, but the strength in my mind, the power within me is the source from where I choose to live and that is something that can never be taken away from me. I'm reaching the end and I can't escape that reality, but I know with all of my being I did all I could and I lived life to the full in every single moment.

When my daughter Phoebe was younger she'd hit a wall within her career, she couldn't decide what road to take, or how she would get there. So, I sat her down and I shared three wise words that someone had once shared with me...

Be Do Have

Who do you need to *be* and what do you need to *do*, in order to *have* exactly what you want. These are some of the most powerful words I've ever heard. The power in realising it really is that simple! You can *be*, you can *do* and you can *have* whatever you want. I know throughout this journey I have done exactly that and wow, I'm grateful for it all.

My family had a strong, powerful belief in me and the fight I'd put up. They refused to just admit defeat. They knew how far we'd come. Giving up now and accepting three days wasn't an option for them. Niamh needed to travel back from Switzerland, where she now lived. The immense pain she must have felt, bless her, getting that call and gathering her stuff to rush to the airport for the earliest flight available - the thought of it brings me so much sadness. They begged for more time, getting the doctor to agree to administer strong antibiotics to buy us more time, which luckily, he did. And three days turned into seven weeks. Seven whole weeks…..

GOODBYES ARE ONLY FOR THOSE WHO LOVE WITH THIER EYES. BECAUSE FOR THOSE WHO LOVE WITH HEART AND SOUL THERE IS NO SUCH THING AS SEPARATION

RUMI

CHAPTER ELEVEN

Seven weeks …….. seven weeks that felt so long but at the same time too short. Not enough time. I need more time. I'm not finished with all I want to do. There is more I need to do. Friends visit each day when I'm awake; those goodbyes are hard. We laugh and joke, sharing memories of the old days, sharing stories of our adventures and tales of what we'd done together. It is a sad time but deeply precious to me, important to me to make time and hold space for those moments I needed with some of my greatest friends. It's important for them too, some of them are friends I've known since the age of 15 and now I'm 59. That's a lifetime of friendship. So, for them, and for me, it is important to have that time together, to sit and laugh about the old days, to look at one another with a quiet acceptance, knowing it's the last "*until next time, mate!*" That's the funny thing with time, we just see it as a given. We think we're entitled to it, but we're not. Time is so, so unpredictable. I spent so many years believing that if I worked hard, when I was older, I could retire and do all the things I had planned. I would travel, I would learn, I would teach, I would share with others my knowledge of the years. I was forgetting that time is not guaranteed, not for any of us.

My hospital bed is now in our living room. My children have all moved in to see this through together, as we'd promised. Nurses come in every day to change my morphine drive. Everything is hazy, I find myself getting confused easily. I'm in an endless cycle, I sleep, I wake, I sleep, I wake. Where's Leo gone? He was just with me, I'm sure of it, so where is he now? Or was I dreaming? Is he dreaming too? Is that how we'll be together now, through a sleepy, dusky sky, meeting somewhere new, somewhere we've never been before? Is that what is to come? The closest I can get to you is only in our dreams. I call out for him and look to my side to see Phoebe sitting by my bed, stroking my head. "Shhhh, it's all right, Dad. We're here, you're not on your own, you're safe, I promise. Go back to sleep."

I drift, I sleep, I dream. I drift, I sleep, I dream.

These seven weeks with my family are hard to explain, a mix of so many emotions. There were times they would lie with me in my hospital bed at home and cry quietly whilst holding my hand. There were times I would wake and we'd laugh and make jokes, almost forgetting what we were doing there. We'd forget how many hours, days, weeks, we'd sat together waiting for the inevitable. We'd watch film after film, although I'd often nod off for most of it. We'd have meal after meal, wondering if that would be my last. When would my ability to eat with my family be ripped away? And I use these words in such a raw way, as that is how it is. Basic functions the human body can perform are taken away in a moment. Your ability to do things unaided is gone. Your freedom, just like that, disappears.

When we started the end of life journey, my family and I made a promise that I would never be alone in the room. One of my five family members would always be next to me. I sobbed with each of them, opening my heart. I didn't want to die alone and I was scared, it crushed me to see the pain my children felt. They had to watch me, their dad, their invincible, untouchable, oh so strong dad, sob and admit his fear of what's to come. It was immensely sad for them all. If they could have sacrificed themselves in that moment and taken the fear and pain for me, I know they all would have in a heartbeat.

Those seven weeks we shared are something that I could never fully explain. The pain, the heartache, the deep, deep sadness, are things we cannot remove from our hearts. These are emotions imprinted on me and my family and even as destructive as they were, they represent a time we would go back to in a heartbeat. It was a time the six of us shared all the love we were capable of, a time my children stepped up to care for me and hold and love their mum, a time they showed nothing but support for one another, a time each of them could show every part of their soul in the rawest form and be received in complete acceptance of utter love and compassion. The way Sue and I had raised them had almost, unknowingly, prepared them for this moment. They held one another fully and would not let go until we had reached the end together.

TO LIVE IN HEARTS WE LEAVE BEHIND IS NOT TO DIE

THOMAS CAMPBELL

CHAPTER TWELVE

By the end of the seven weeks, I am nothing more than a shell, no part of me looks like me any longer. My body no longer has anything left to give. Although I'm no longer awake, I hear everything. Each breath is a struggle, just a wheezing sound from my throat. I cry, I cry, I cry inside with deep sadness. All my family can see on my face is the expression of utter devastation. I'm leaving. It's time. After all we've done for three years, after all we've battled, all we've conquered, everything we've overcome, it's time. The pull is too strong. My body is so, so weak. I can no longer win against what I've fought so hard to beat.

I drift, I sleep, I dream. I drift, I sleep, I dream.

In a dreamy haze I remember all those who have impacted my life, all those who have made my life so rich with love. Memories flow back to me that are full of an abundance of gratitude, like whispers in the night sky.

I think of my two grandsons, Leo and Gabriel, my heart shattering into a million pieces. I love those boys. What they gave me in the short time I had with them both is more than anyone could have ever imagined, the gift to carry on, to be strong, and the gift of peace, the gift to let go.

Why didn't we have more time? There's so much I wanted to teach them both, so much I wanted to share with them, share with all of them, my step-grandchildren and those I never got to meet too. We just never got the time I truly thought we'd always have.

To all my grandchildren, wherever you go know that I'm always right behind you, holding you, supporting you and loving you every day. I love you all, from every space in my heart.

My children, my four amazing children. Wow, what a gift you've been. I feel overwhelmed with gratitude for the life we walked together. I feel honoured to have been your father in this lifetime. My boys, you're so strong, you have my power, my passion, my fire don't forget it and my darling girls, I'm so proud of the women you've grown up to be, you both inspire me, it's incredible, I love you. I love you all so much. I'm so deeply proud of you all that my heart bursts with pride. Thank you for it all, what an epic time we had. Hold on to all those memories we made, keep them close to your heart, that's where you'll find me, I'm never far. I love you all so, so much.

My son-in-law, Chris and my daughter-in-law's, Lisa and Jodie. Thank you for loving my family, thank you for holding us every day and all the days to come. The compassion, care and softness you hold for my children and myself overwhelms my heart with joy. I know you'll look after them all and one another.

My mum, you gave me it all and WOW, what a gift. You gave me this life and for that my gratitude to you will remain for eternity. I'll no longer be in pain. You no longer need to watch me suffer. Please know I'm at peace, it's OK, I'm OK, everything will be OK. I love you mum.

My sisters, Paula, Lisa, Kim and Christine, what a journey. The memories we share stay alive forever. Nothing can break what we shared and we will continue to share. I'm there guiding you, loving you, as always. I'm never far from you.

My brother-in-law, Kev, thank you for the complete devotion you gave to me over all the years, especially the end. Your love, kindness and generosity are your most precious qualities. Thank you for standing by my family's side, I know you'll take care of them. I love you mate.

My most trusted friends, you know who you are. A lifetime of friendship and what a ride it was. The laughter, the tears, I loved it all. So deeply blessed to have shared my life with you all. The memories we made will stay with me forever, I love you all, I really do.

My fellow foodie, fueled with the same passion and deep gratitude for food, Celia. Thank you for creating the vision of Heart Kitchen with me, my final project and one I am so happy I got to fulfil. Keep cooking from your heart and know that when you do, I'm right by your side.

My surgeon, Kito, my oncologists, Justin and Dan, my

dietician, Jane, and all the medical teams that have supported me through my journey, thank you! Without you all I would have never met my grandsons. I would have missed out on so many precious moments with my family. My gratitude to you all will remain firmly in my heart, thank you.

My family and friends. Guys, where do I start? You empowered me with so much strength, you really did. The belief you all held for me was a power in itself, as well as the support, the love, the deep, deep care. I cannot thank you all enough. To know I leave this earth with my family in your hands and hearts gives me the greatest sense of completion. I know you've got them. I know you've got each other. Remember all I said, all I shared, all I taught you. Share that with the world, share that for me, I love you all. Thank you!

And the hardest to leave, my darling Sue. My beautiful soulmate, I was so blessed to have shared my life with you. What a gift you've been to me. What power you gave me, what devotion, what love. The children you gave us, the life you helped us to build, just thank you. I adore you beyond measure. Please do all the things we wanted to do, travel the world, embrace every opportunity, don't let the fire burn out in my absence as I'm right by your side embracing it all. I'll stay by your side, as I promised, you'll know I'm never far. I'm with you sweetheart, at every sunrise over the woodland, at every moment of heartache, I'm there, I love you Beary.

Glimmers of gold glow float from my body, flying

softly to somewhere new. I am so calm, so peaceful, surrounded by my family, wrapped in memories that I've made with all those I love. Taking every treasured moment with me, holding all those gifts firmly within my heart.

I drift, I sleep, I dream. I drift, I sleep, I dream. I drift, I sleep, I sleep, I sleep...... I leave....

AND IN THE END, IT'S NOT THE YEARS IN A LIFE, IT'S THE LIFE IN THE YEARS

ABRAHAM LINCLON

THE END – THE WHITE SANDS OF HEAVEN

Back on the beach where this story begun, I stand on the pure white sand, feeling the ground beneath me, feeling my feet covered by the grit of the sand, hearing the soft sound of the pure blue ocean. The sea hums a gentle song to me, a song that gives me comfort, I feel at home with it. I look out ahead and see all whom I love across the crystal water. The laughter and the love they have between them fills every space in my heart with utter joy. I look down to my feet and I see my grandchildren building their creations in the sand.

I look at my body, it doesn't feel like mine. I feel for my scars, but the wounds from my journey in life have faded. I run my hands across my bones and they are no longer grasping on to fat as they had done before. I no longer feel weak. "I am strong." I stand and breathe. I think to myself, "It's OK, Simon." I know that right now in this moment, is exactly where I'm meant to be.

I take a deep breath. I feel the warmth in the air. I know that my journey in life has come to an end. I didn't want it to but I know it's a truth I can no longer escape from. Almost three years of a painful, yet beautiful, journey have passed. I'm scared but somehow, I feel at peace. I know I have built a foundation of love and strength, between myself and my family; something so incredible that, in my absence, now I am gone, the love I've created will live on. My grandson, Leo, always says to me "Come on,

Grandpa. You can make it!' These words have never seemed so clear to me. In this moment, I realise, I have made it…. I am free.

**THERE ARE SOME WHO BRING A LIGHT
SO GREAT TO THE WORLD THAT EVEN
AFTER THEY HAVE GONE THE LIGHT
REMAINS**

UNKNOWN

MY FINAL WORD

Thank you for being a part of my journey. Thank you for listening to my story, a story I always wanted to share. Use it as a lesson, if you will. Time is not a given, life is not a given. Do everything you want, everything you desire, do it all, whilst you still can. Stare up to the starry sky and watch the sparkle shine from within each star. Take a deep breath, feel the breath. Feel the gratitude for all the memories and moments you've been able to make with those you love most. Look for the gifts, there are so many. The earth is a magical place… if you take time to notice.

Until we meet again,

Simon x

I AM FREE

Written by Simon Gale - Channeled by Phoebe Young

In the morning, when I am not here, please don't
panic, there's no need to fear,

The worlds we live in are different now, I'm not sure I
can tell you, but I can show you how,

Allow yourself to dream with me, close your eyes and
you will see,

I'm a part of you, I'm all around, you'll hear me in the
wind, you'll hear me in its sound,

The way we'll speak is different now, but it's
something I taught you I know you know how,

Use your heart and I will hear, trust yourself, don't fall
to the fear, remember the words, the words from me,
do not feel sad, for now, I am free.

THE PRAYER OF ST. FRANCIS

Lord, make me an instrument of your peace;
Where there is hatred, let me sow love;
Where there is injury, pardon;
Where there is doubt, faith;
Where there is despair, hope;
Where there is darkness, light;
And where there is sadness, joy.

O Divine Master,
Grant that I may not so much seek
To be consoled as to console;
To be understood, as to understand;
To be loved, as to love;
For it is in giving that we receive,
It is in pardoning that we are pardoned,
And it is in dying that we are born to Eternal Life.

Amen.

SIMON'S RECIPE

From our day in Heart Kitchen

Homemade Tagliatelle & Slow Slow Slow Ox Cheek Ragu……. Lento, Lento, Lento Guancia di Bue Ragu con Tagliatelle

By Simon Gale

Ingredients for ragu
2 medium ox cheeks or another meat of your choice
Large handful root vegetables
1 to 2 splashes of delicious Italian red wine
1 medium carrot
1 medium celery stick
1 medium onion
1 tbsp tomato purée
50g smoked pancetta
Dash of salt and pepper
6 tbsps. double cream
1 small truffle

Ingredients for pasta
100gpasta flour
1 medium egg
1 large HEART full of love - send that love to your pasta!

Directions

FOR THE SLOW COOKED OX CHEEK

Slow roast seasoned ox cheeks on a bed of the roughly chopped root vegetables, adding red wine, and slow cook for 8 hours - SLOW SLOW SLOW - 120c ..... imagine when these little bad boys are ready, they swell up to double their original size........it's like eating clouds!

FOR THE RAGU

Once your ox cheeks are slow roasted, infused and looking beautiful, you can start on your ragu. Firstly, you want to make a soffritto. Melt a little butter and fry the all vegetables and pancetta for 5-6 minutes, stirring constantly. Add the ox cheeks - breaking them up slightly - and stir together so it can infuse. Add the diluted tomato purée to the sticky juices left in the roasting pan from the meat, stir to de-glaze and add to the ragu, de-glazing really helps with the washing up!! Season with salt and pepper. Stir thoroughly, TASTE - TASTE - TASTE, adjust, cover and leave to simmer very slowly for a minimum of 2 hours. During this time, ensure the ragu does not dry out, you need to stir it every so often, adding warm water if necessary. To finish, add the cream and shaved truffle.
NOTE: extend the cooking time as per the slow roasting.

FOR THE TAGLIATELLE

MAKING FRESH PASTA ...... vision and being...who do we need to be and what do we need to do to support that being to have the most wonderful pasta? Let's build a vision right now.....from pure imagination......"I notice the heat of the sun on my skin, aromas fill the air, fresh tomatoes and basil grow in pots around me. My face is alive with excitement and anticipation. I see my bin of flour and my hands are eager to get working. I feel the strength in my fingers and the love in my heart. Three simple everyday ingredients, water, flour and eggs, come together to create an amazing, hearty and wholesome food. I plunge my hands into the flour, take out enormous handfuls, it feels soft and light to my fingers. Grabbing my jug of water, I mix steadily to form my dough. I begin to work it and feel the muscles in my arms striving as I move, bringing it all together. I am aware of a thought, it's "wow! they've been making this since ancient times, exactly the same way!" I feel my heart expand with joy and love as I hold my silky, smooth pasta dough in my hands.

Try this, it's simple, grab a handful of basil and smell it, play some Italian music and I bet you it will transport you to Italy to be the passionate Italian cook.

For every person eating you will need 1 egg and 100g(4oz) of pasta flour. Bear in mind that no 2 batches of flour are identical and that no 2 eggs are ever quite the same size - so if you do end up having to add another egg or extra flour to your mixture it's no problem, it is not an indication of failure on your part! I do feel that trying to explain in writing how to make fresh pasta is very hard to do and must be almost impossible to really grasp for the reader. It's far better to go to a pasta making class if you can, so that you can see for yourself what actually happens during this magical process!

So, let's begin! Put all the flour in a pile on your work surface and plunge your fist into the centre to make a hollow. Break your eggs into the hole and add a pinch of salt. Using your fingers or a fork, beat the eggs thoroughly, don't worry if the flour starts to mix in. Begin to roughly knead the flour and bring it all together and continue kneading. This is not like making pastry, so this is not the moment for a delicate approach, but on the other hand if you are too heavy handed you will cause the dough to dry out too much and it won't roll out smoothly.

Keep kneading until you have a smooth, pliable ball of dough. Rest the dough in cling film for an hour, this makes it a lot more manageable.

Now comes the hard part. Sprinkle your surface with some semolina to avoid any sticking and roll out your dough as thinly as possible with a strong, long rolling pin. Continue to roll it over and over again until your dough is really elastic, smooth and shiny. It should cool down considerably as you work it, and you will feel the temperature dropping as you go along. When it is ready, the sheet of dough will feel like brand new, wrung out, damp chamois leather, but it must not be brittle. TIP- keep it damp when not working it with a damp cloth and keep it on a floured surface.

Alternatively, you can use a pasta machine instead of the traditional rolling pin. Take your dough and break off a piece about the size of a small fist. Flatten this section out and with your hand push it through the widest setting on your pasta machine. Fold this in half and repeat. Do this 3 times. Now move your machine down to the next setting. Repeat the feeding and folding process another 3 times. Continue in this rhythm, moving your setting down every 3 times until you hear the pasta snap as if it was going through rollers. At this point, you can forget about folding it in half every time, as the surface tension is now perfect. Continue to wind it through the rollers to the last or penultimate setting on the machine, depending on how fine you want your pasta. Lay the pasta sheet carefully onto a floured surface. Then repeat this whole process with another lump of dough, placing every finished piece carefully onto the floured side as it will be very delicate.

Once all the rolling is done, you can then cut your pasta into any desired shape, be it sheets, tagliatelle, ravioli etc. You can cook your pasta immediately for around 3-5 minutes. If you are making ravioli, remember to keep your pasta moist as the pasta case will not seal and close if too dry. In this case, fill your parcels first, seal and then leave to dry. You can freeze any extra dough for up to 1 month, just bag it up, label and enjoy whenever you're in the Italian mood!

To make tagliatelle ribbons, either switch your pasta machine to tagliatelle cutter or roll out the dough whisper-thin and slice into ribbons.

In a large pan of salted boiling water, cook the fresh pasta for 3 minutes or until " al dente ", i.e. cooked but still slightly firm to the bite.

In a beautiful bowl, put some of your fresh, full-of-love pasta, a few large spoonful's of your delicious mouth-watering ragu and add a small handful of fresh parsley and a sprinkle of parmesan cheese! Homemade tagliatelle & slow, slow, slow ox cheek ragu, bellissimo!

∞∞∞∞

For more of Simon's recipes visit

www.heartkitchen.co.uk

thank you

Mum
Without your help this book wouldn't of become possible. I'm beyond grateful for you.

My husband Chris
You gave me your time and wisdom fully, and I am so grateful for that.

To my children
You inspire me daily to be the best version of myself, I love you all.

Family & Friends
Your support and love goes above and beyond. I'm so blessed to have you all.

Lastly, My Dad Thank you!
Thank you for lessons, the love, the light. My life feels less whole without you here and my world may be different, but the gifts you've left behind will be ones I embrace every day.

Be, Do, Have.
I love you Dad, Endlessly.